LET'S GET A PET!

MY FIRST BIRD

By Joan Stoltman

Gareth Stevens PUBLISHING

Please visit our website, www.garethstevens.com. For a free color catalog of all our high-quality books, call toll free 1-800-542-2595 or fax 1-877-542-2596.

Cataloging-in-Publication Data

Names: Stoltman, Joan.
Title: My first bird / Joan Stoltman.
Description: New York : Gareth Stevens Publishing, 2018. | Series: Let's get a pet!| Includes index.
Identifiers: ISBN 9781482464375 (pbk.) | ISBN 9781482464399 (library bound) | ISBN 9781482464382 (6 pack)
Subjects: LCSH: Cage birds–Juvenile literature. | Birds–Juvenile literature.
Classification: LCC SF461.35 S76 2018 | DDC 636.6'8–dc23

Published in 2018 by
Gareth Stevens Publishing
111 East 14th Street, Suite 349
New York, NY 10003

Designer: Bethany Perl
Editor: Joan Stoltman

Photo credits: p. 1 Alena Ozerova/Shutterstock.com; pp. 2–24 (background texture) Liliya Mulyukova/Shutterstock.com; p. 5 BestPhotoStudio/Shutterstock.com; pp 7, 17 Zurijeta/ Shutterstock.com; p. 9 Rosa Jay/Shutterstock.com; p. 11 Dorling Kindersley/Getty Images; p. 13 dorglao/Shutterstock.com; p. 15 victorass/Shutterstock.com; p. 19 Viktor Prymachenko/ Shutterstock.com; p. 21 Krunja/Shutterstock.com.

Printed in China

CPSIA compliance information: Batch #CS17GS: For further information contact Gareth Stevens, New York, New York at 1-800-542-2595.

CONTENTS

Boldface words appear in the glossary.

Feathered Friends

Birds are so interesting! Their feathers are made of the same thing as your fingernails. They have a **beak**, a built-in tool used for finding and eating food, climbing, and much more. They stand all day, even during sleep. What a cool pet to have!

A Bird's Day

Just like you, birds start their day with breakfast! When everyone goes to school and work, it's time to sleep. When everyone comes home, they wake up to play and eat dinner. Then it's time to sleep again! Birds sleep around 12 hours a day.

Food

Many birds are also a lot like you because they need fresh fruits and vegetables every day. Different types of birds have different **diets**. Ask your bird's **veterinarian** which bird food and snacks are good for your bird.

Preening and Cleaning

It's easy to keep your pet bird clean because they do most of the work! Birds **preen** themselves every day with their beak. Plus, they love to bathe in water! No towels are needed—they dry themselves!

Cage Setup

Birdcages come in many sizes because pet birds can be big, small, or somewhere in between! Ask for help when buying a cage. Your bird will be happiest with its new cage against a wall in the room where your family hangs out the most.

WHAT A BIRD NEEDS

Birds are a lot of work to clean up after. There are things you can do every day to help out. Put clean newspaper at the bottom of the cage, and give your bird clean water. Don't forget to clean the floor around your bird's cage, too!

Bird Fun

Birds need to be played with every day. You can teach them tricks, like high fives or shaking hands. Or you can just talk! That will make them happy, too! Birds also love to listen to the radio and TV.

Keeping Your Bird Safe

It's fun to allow your pet bird out of the cage. Before you let it out, make sure all doors and windows are closed so that it doesn't fly away. Always watch a pet bird when it's out of its cage to make sure it stays safe.

What's in a Name?

Naming your pet is one of the greatest parts of pet **ownership**! You can name your pet anything, from your favorite TV or book character to a silly sound! Some popular names for birds include Charlie, Coco, Angel, Kiwi, Polly, Tweety, and Birdy.

GLOSSARY

beak: the bill of a bird

diet: the food an animal eats

ownership: the state of owning something

preen: to groom, or clean, feathers

veterinarian: a doctor who is trained to treat animals

FOR MORE INFORMATION

BOOKS

Gardeski, Christina Mia. *Pet Birds: Questions and Answers.* North Mankato, MN: Capstone Press, 2017.

Mead, Wendy. *Kids Top 10 Pet Birds.* Berkeley Heights, NJ: Enslow Elementary, 2015.

Meister, Cari. *Birds.* Minneapolis, MN: Bullfrog Books, 2015.

WEBSITES

Birds
ducksters.com/animals/birds.php
Find facts and information about everything bird related!

Fun Parrot Facts for Kids
sciencekids.co.nz/sciencefacts/animals/parrot.html
Read fun parrot facts!

PBS Kids Go! Taking Care of Your Pet
pbskids.org/itsmylife/family/pets/article7.html
Learn general tips about what all pets need.

Publisher's note to educators and parents: Our editors have carefully reviewed these websites to ensure that they are suitable for students. Many websites change frequently, however, and we cannot guarantee that a site's future contents will continue to meet our high standards of quality and educational value. Be advised that students should be closely supervised whenever they access the Internet.

INDEX